Teacher's Guide and Novel Unit for Hello, Universe

By:

John Pennington

The lessons on demand series is designed to provide ready to use resources for novel study. In this book you will find key vocabulary, student organizer pages, and assessments.

This guide is divided into two sections. Section one is the teacher section which consists of vocabulary and activities. Section two holds all of the student pages, including assessments and graphic organizers.

Now available! Student Workbooks!

Section One

Teacher Pages

Vocabulary

Suggested Activities

Chapter 1-13 Vocabulary

Hurdle

Anvil

Posture

Exception

Exhibit

Routine

Unison

Perpetually

Urgency

Zodiac

Notorious

Debilitate

Chapters 1-13 Activities

Reading Check Question / Quiz:

Who did Virgil seek advice from? Kaori Tanaka

Who was the target from Virgil's "Grand Failure?" Valencia

Who is the Tiger of Elm Street? Chet Bullens

What color is Virgil warned to beware? Red

Blooms Higher Order Question:

Create a character "web" linking characters and how they are connected.

Suggested Activity Sheets (see Section Two):

Character Sketch—Virgil

Character Sketch—Valencia

Character Sketch—Kaori

Character Sketch—Lola

Character Sketch—Gulliver

Research Connection—Zoology

Research Connection—Jane Goodall

Draw the Scene

Who, What, When, Where and How

Chapter 14-24 Vocabulary

Sparse

Assertive

Ominous

Receded

Evidence

Antagonize

Interfere

Predicted

Hyperventilate

Nomad

Inherit

Punctual

Chapters 14-24 Activities

Reading Check Question / Quiz:

What did Virgil take with him into the woods? Backpack and Gulliver

What did Chet take from Virgil? Backpack

Who does Valencia take food? Sacred

What did Virgil need to do that he had never done before? Yell

Blooms Higher Order Question:

Compose a map of the area and the path that each character walks.

Suggested Activity Sheets (see Section Two):

Character Sketch—Chet

Character Sketch—Sacred

Character Sketch—Joselito

Character Sketch—Julius

Research Connection—Constellations

Research Connection—Archaeology

Precognition Sheet

What Would You Do?

Chapters 25-End Vocabulary

Embodied

Unconscious

Anxious

Vigor

Intimidate

Enigma

Perceptive

Nonchalant

Heritage

Suffocate

Atrocious

Emerge

Chapter 25-End Activities

Reading Check Question / Quiz:

Who attacks Virgil while he is in the well? Pah

What is Valencia afraid of? Being alone

Why is Chet in the woods? Looking for a snake

What item allows Virgil to escape? Gen's Jump Rope

Blooms Higher Order Question:

Develop an summary for each chapter.

Suggested Activity Sheets (see Section Two):

Character Sketch—Gen

Character Sketch—Pah

Character Sketch—Paulito

Character Sketch—Ruby San Salvador

Research Connection—How to handle snakes

Research Connection—Heredity

Create the Test

Interview

Top Ten List—Events

Write a Letter

Chapter Vocabulary

Chapter Activities

Reading Check Question / Quiz:

Blooms Higher Order Question:

Suggested Activity Sheets (see Section Two):

Discussion Questions

Section Two

Student Work Pages

Work Pages

Graphic Organizers

Assessments

Activity Descriptions

Advertisement—Select an item from the text and have the students use text clues to draw an advertisement about that item.

Chapter to Poem—Students select 20 words from the text to write a five line poem with 3 words on each line.

Character Sketch—Students complete the information about a character using text clues.

Comic Strip— Students will create a visual representation of the chapter in a series of drawings.

Compare and Contrast—Select two items to make relationship connections with text support.

Create the Test—have the students use the text to create appropriate test questions.

Draw the Scene—students use text clues to draw a visual representation of the chapter.

Interview— Students design questions you would ask a character in the book and then write that characters response.

Lost Scene—Students use text clues to decide what would happen after a certain place in the story.

Making Connections—students use the text to find two items that are connected and label what kind of relationship connects them.

Precognition Sheet—students envision a character, think about what will happen next, and then determine what the result of that would be.

Activity Descriptions

Pyramid—Students use the text to arrange a series of items in an hierarchy format.

Research Connection—Students use an outside source to learn more about a topic in the text.

Sequencing—students will arrange events in the text in order given a specific context.

Support This! - Students use text to support a specific idea or concept.

Travel Brochure—Students use information in the text to create an informational text about the location

Top Ten List—Students create a list of items ranked from 1 to 10 with a specific theme.

Vocabulary Box—Students explore certain vocabulary words used in the text.

What Would You Do? - Students compare how characters in the text would react and compare that with how they personally would react.

Who, What, When, Where, and How—Students create a series of questions that begin with the following words that are connected to the text.

Write a Letter—Students write a letter to a character in the text.

Activity Descriptions (for scripts and poems)

Add a Character—Students will add a character that does not appear in the scene and create dialog and responses from other characters.

Costume Design—Students will design costumes that are appropriate to the characters in the scene and explain why they chose the design.

Props Needed— Students will make a list of props they believe are needed and justify their choices with text.

Soundtrack! - Students will create a sound track they believe fits the play and justify each song choice.

Stage Directions— Students will decide how the characters should move on, around, or off stage.

Poetry Analysis—Students will determine the plot, theme, setting, subject, tone and important words and phrases.

NAME:

TEACHER:

Date:

Advertisement: Draw an advertisement for the book

NAME:

TEACHER:

Date:

Chapter to Poem

Assignment: Select 20 words found in the chapter to create a poem where each line is 3 words long.

Title:

_____   _____   _____

_____   _____   _____

_____   _____   _____

_____   _____   _____

_____   _____   _____

NAME:

TEACHER:

Date:

Character Sketch

Name

Draw a picture

Personality/ Distinguishing marks

Connections to other characters

Important Actions

NAME:

TEACHER:

Date:

Comic Strip

Compare and Contrast

Venn Diagram

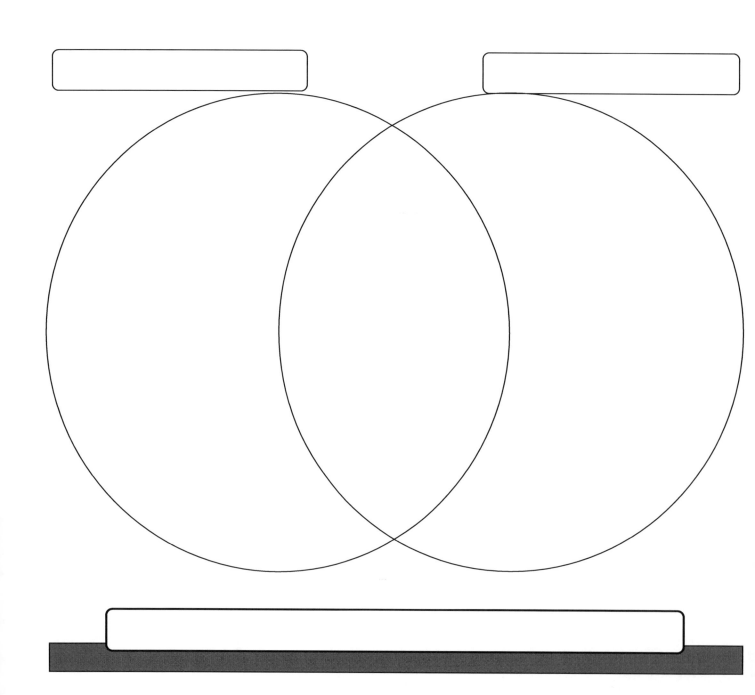

NAME:

Create the Test

Question:

Answer:

Question:

Answer:

Question:

Answer:

Question:

Answer:

Draw the Scene: What five things have you included in the scene?

1

2

3

4

5

NAME:

TEACHER:

Date:

Interview: Who _____

Question:

Answer:

Question:

Answer:

Question:

Answer:

Question:

Answer:

NAME:

TEACHER:

Date:

Lost Scene: Write a scene that takes place between _____ and

_____

Making Connections

What is the connection?

NAME:

TEACHER:

Date:

Precognition Sheet

Who ?

What's going to happen?

What will be the result?

Who ?

What's going to happen?

What will be the result?

Who ?

What's going to happen?

What will be the result?

Who ?

What's going to happen?

What will be the result?

How many did you get correct?

NAME:

TEACHER:

Date:

Assignment: Pyramid

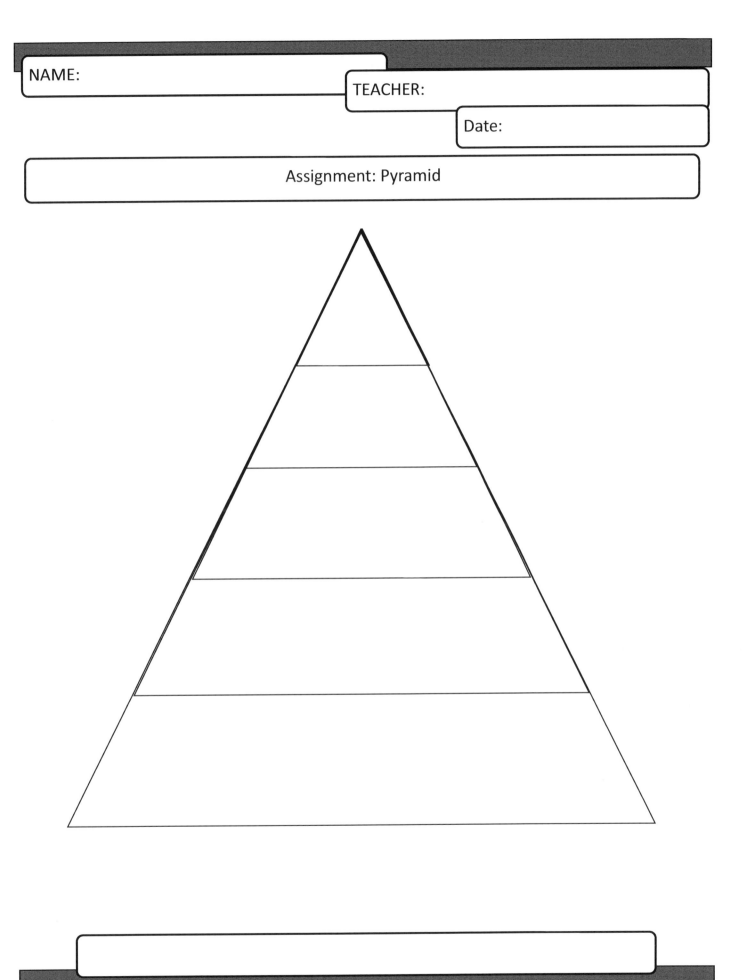

NAME:

TEACHER:

Date:

Research connections

Source (URL, Book, Magazine, Interview)

What am I researching?

Facts I found that could be useful or notes

1.

2.

3.

4.

5.

6.

NAME:

TEACHER:

Date:

Sequencing
or timeline

1.

2.

3.

4.

5.

NAME:

TEACHER:

Date:

Support This!

Supporting text

What page?

Supporting text

What page?

Central idea or statement

_____

Supporting text

What page?

Supporting text

What page?

NAME:

TEACHER:

Date:

Travel Brochure

Why should you visit?

Map

What are you going to see?

Special Events

Top Ten List

1.

2.

3.

4.

5.

6.

7.

8.

9.

10.

NAME:

TEACHER:

Date:

Vocabulary Box

Definition:

Draw:

Word:

Related words:

Use in a sentence:

Definition:

Draw:

Word:

Related words:

Use in a sentence:

NAME:

TEACHER:

Date:

What would you do?

Character: _____

What did they do?

Example from text:

What would you do?

Why would that be better?

Character: _____

What did they do?

Example from text:

What would you do?

Why would that be better?

Character: _____

What did they do?

Example from text:

What would you do?

Why would that be better?

NAME:

TEACHER:

Date:

Who, What, When, Where, and How

Who

What

Where

When

How

NAME:

TEACHER:

Date:

Write a letter

To:

From:

NAME:

TEACHER:

Date:

Assignment:

Add a Character

Who is the new character?

What reason does the new character have for being there?

Write a dialog between the new character and characters currently in the scene.

You dialog must be 6 lines or more, and can occur in the beginning, middle or end of the scene.

Costume Design

Draw a costume for one the characters in the scene.

Why do you believe this character should have a costume like this?

NAME:

TEACHER:

Date:

Props Needed

Prop:

What text from the scene supports this?

Prop:

What text from the scene supports this?

Prop:

What text from the scene supports this?

NAME:

TEACHER:

Date:

Soundtrack!

Song:

Why should this song be used?

Song:

Why should this song be used?

Song:

Why should this song be used?

NAME:

TEACHER:

Date:

Stage Directions

List who is moving, how they are moving and use text from the dialog to determine when they move.

Who:

How:

When:

Who:

How:

When:

Who:

How:

When:

NAME:

TEACHER:

Date:

Poetry Analysis

Name of Poem:

Subject:

Text Support:

Plot:

Text Support:

Theme:

Text Support:

Setting:

Text Support:

Tone:

Text Support:

Important Words and Phrases:

Why are these words and phrases important:

48174609R00026

Made in the USA
Lexington, KY
15 August 2019